# The Last Normal Year

Kevin Murphy

Sidekick Press
Bellingham, Washington

Publisher's Note: This is a work of fiction. Names, characters, places, and incidents are a product of the author's imagination. Locales and public names are sometimes used for atmospheric purposes. Any resemblance to actual people, living or dead, or to businesses, companies, events, institutions, or locales is completely coincidental.

Published 2025
Printed in the United States of America
ISBN: 978-1-958808-39-9
LCCN: 2024950500

Sidekick Press
2950 Newmarket Street, Suite 101-329
Bellingham, Washington 98226
sidekickpress.com

*The Last Normal Year*

Cover design by Coral Black

# Praise for *The Last Normal Year*

With "poetry and bedazzlement for all," Kevin Murphy inspires our allegiance to "the state of trance and / wonderment, and to the myriad manifestations which it engenders." This collection is a riotous and resplendent celebration—a curious and searching exploration—a cacophony of beauty. It is a gift summoned by a poet's heart from the ether to pull us from the humdrum woes of an overburdened planet and lift us toward the magnificence of possibility innate to our human existence. *The Last Normal Year* will add an abnormal sparkle to your day.

—Rena Priest, Washington State Poet Laureate (2021-2023)

There's a wild and unfettered imagination at play in these rambling verses, which find their inspiration from the farthest galaxy all the way down to the poet's bare foot, from the man who falls in love with a crab apple tree to the speaker's many lives as a fly. Take a look at "The Buddha Rat Blues," take a listen to "First Guitar," check out *The Last Normal Year*!

—Joseph Millar, author of *Shine*

*The Last Normal Year* makes me wish I could do a loud, two-fingers-in-the-mouth whistle that says, "Hurry! Look at this!" With panache and wisdom informed by Lorca, J.S. Bach, Allen Ginsberg, the Buddha, Whitman, Bob Dylan, Jesus, Wikipedia, and Dr. Seuss, among others, Murphy's poems make the absurd feel holy and vice versa. Small, unremarkable objects—yam, bean, carrot, rock—are elevated to unexpected glory, while big ideas—culture, normalcy, God—are paraded in all their finery. And the lists! Murphy's menagerie includes weasel, yak, camel, dung beetle, chihuahua, cockroach, marmoset, macaw, rat, and many monkeys (some, arguably, human). Readable and energetic, with a spoken-word drive, Kevin Murphy is the poet you want as your tour guide to the land of absurdity. "God said: let there be a lack of proper seriousness / and there was a lack of proper seriousness." Yep. (Loud whistle.)

—J.I. Kleinberg, author of *The Word for Standing Alone in a Field* (Bottlecap Press) and *Sleeping Lessons* (Milk & Cake Press)

Kevin Murphy's poems can bring out the twinkle on a mosquito's ankles and grant a PhD to a wildebeest. What I mean is, his poems accomplish marvelous things that poems by most other poets don't. He always welcomes the natural genius of the reader, and whether the poems are heard on the stage or read on the page, they are always, in the best ways, participatory events.

—James Bertolino, author of *Every Wound Has a Rhythm*, *Pocket Animals*, and *Snail River*

for Jeannie

# CONTENTS

section one

# My Extended Family

My extended family transcends barriers of species, phyla, order,
　　and class
Sprawls across genomes, kingdoms, and continents
My extended family comprises not only every one of the
　　multitudinous Murphys of Ireland
Not only the entire sprawling clan of neo-Gothic affiliates on my
　　maternal side
But all humanoids without regard to race, creed or socio-economic
　　status
Horse thieves, drunkards, and scoundrels of every stripe
Apes, both illiterate and erudite
Toads, hyenas, jackals, and vultures
Sea slugs and ponderosa pines
Wolf lichen and thimbleberries

Long-lost cousins chortle in the shrubbery or hang screeching in
　　caves
Impromptu family reunions occur at murky river bottoms
Where the catfish are uncles, the eels are aunties
And the river itself is the great-great-grandmother

My extended family includes
1500 species of rodent, 350 thousand different kinds of beetles, 20
　　thousand varieties of flatworm, the spores of extraterrestrial
　　slime mold, and as much as it pains me to admit it, all 435
　　members of the US House of Representatives
My family straddles the microbial/mineral divide
We gyrate under microscopes and gnaw the bones of dead sheep
　　by candlelight
We are clingy, foamy, bedraggled and lumpy
Atomically unstable and emotionally volatile

But whatever our issues, we have always been
A close family
Intimately entangled, if unconsciously so
Bound by an affection that is cellular, even molecular
Co-conspirators in the convoluted collusion sometimes known
As life on planet Earth

# Poem Gone Wrong

something has gone
    terribly wrong with the poem

it no longer responds
    to simple requests
    or commands

the poem that could once
    do the work of seven novels
    hold the dreams of seven cities
        turn every argument
into a song
    now sleeps until noon
    spits out a few greasy syllables
        and calls it a day
if you suggest
    it could use its superpowers
    for the good of all sentient beings
it looks at you
    like you're insane

poem, you can see
    what's going on out there
snap out of it, poem
    we need you

# The Blue Jay, the Man, and the Dandelion

Once there was a blue jay, and a man, and a dandelion, and they
    lived together in a poem
Where they enacted various dreamlike scenarios and they explored
    the parameters of mythology and paradox, and they discussed
    politics and art, and all was good
Until one day, the dandelion announced it needed some space, and
    was moving out to start its own poem.

In the new poem, the dandelion god is roaring in the sky, and the
    dandelion god is roaming the savannah, resplendent in its
    golden mane,
And the dandelion god is worshiped for its wine and its root and
    its leaf, its yellow fury and its luminous poof
And the lion is the sun and the sun is the lion, and they are both
    aspects of the dandelion.

And the city calls off the war on weeds, the exterminators shed
    their rubberized suits and their canisters of poison
And they raise their hosannas to the great buttery flower-faced
    wine-drunk god,
And the orchid, the rose, the tulip, and the peony tremble before it,
And the sidewalk gladly fractures to allow the emergence of the
    immortals,
And the air is filled with glorious fluff.

Meanwhile, back in the original poem, the blue jay and the man
    both know the jig is up, but neither wants to write the last line.
Like many poems, theirs is never finished, only abandoned.
Before long, it is completely taken over by morning glories, who,
    needless to say,
Have their own literary ambitions.

# Cézanne's Carrot

*The day is coming when a single carrot, freshly observed, will set off a revolution.*
~Paul Cézanne

you look at the carrot, the carrot looks at you
you zoom in, zoom out
you rotate the carrot
ninety degrees, one-eighty, three-sixty
then you
        spin like a dervish
while the carrot remains still

you grate the carrot, sauté the carrot
you cut the carrot into matchsticks
you burn down the house

you bite the carrot, chew
suck the pulp, swallow the juice, describe the experience
in your notebook

in terms of chocolate and cabernet
in terms of shoe leather and cigar smoke
you bite the carrot, note that the carrot does not bite you back
maybe it's because the carrot is a vegetarian
maybe you're a vegetarian
but that doesn't really help the carrot

you arrange a hundred carrots in a wheel, a mandala, every
carrot pointing to the darkness at the center of the wheel
you meditate on that darkness, lose yourself in it

you look at the paintings of cézanne
you see the men playing poker, a naked woman wading into a
    river, spindly fingers on the brim of a hat
you see wine bottles and piles of plums and apples, a pile of skulls
but no carrots

the day is coming, says paul cézanne
but cézanne has been dead for over a hundred years
what's the story, paul cézanne, are we on the right track?
is the day coming still
or did it come and go without our noticing?

# Animal Spirits

*"Animal spirits" is a term used by John Maynard Keynes . . . to describe the instincts, proclivities, and emotions that seemingly influence human behavior, which can be measured in terms of consumer confidence.*
*~Wikipedia*

The computers—they just want to go to sleep
but the animal spirits won't let them.

A man stands at an ATM fumbling with his credit cards,
    the ghost of a weasel moves in.
Teenagers fall headfirst into their phones,
    when they come out, they're obsessed
by something a moose said in somebody's dream.

The camels and yaks of distant caravans
    drive interest rates over the cliff,
the wings of a monarch butterfly
    lift them up again.
The buying, the spending, the getting, the grabbing—so much
    depends
        on the exhalations of a prehistoric horse,
        the wordless hunger of the dung beetle,
        the all-knowing bones of a red-eyed frog,
        the swishing tail of a kangaroo rat.

The computers—two thousand, two million, five billion
    computers, they're so tired, they just want to go to sleep
but the animal spirits are chattering, belching, cooing,
    hissing.

The animal spirits have worked their way into
    the fiber-optic cables on the ocean floor.
They're sucking the marrow out of the algorithms.
They're gnawing on the zeroes of your bank account.
They're tearing up the insulation
    that separates order from oblivion.

Most financial experts project
that sometime in the upcoming fiscal year,
animal spirits will recover their bodies.
When they do, they will come to your house
when you least expect it,
and when it is least convenient,
they will come,

and they will eat you.

# On the Varieties of Religious Experience

according to some, jesus
    is the pilot of a pimped-out flying saucer
according to some, jesus
    plays fiddle like a fiend possessed
according to some, jesus
    is a peyote button, or a
mustard seed, or a viking disguised
    as a movie star, or a ghost
trapped in a cement overcoat
    or a fish superimposed
on a pyramid, meanwhile
    the historical jesus sits up all night
in the darkest room
    of the blue hotel, wondering
why no one ever comes to visit
    because jesus is jesus
even as he sits on the bed
    he is also
healing the sick in pittsburgh
    and when he is in the mojave desert
eating nothing-burgers with devils
    he is at that same moment
ordering fries at a booth in baltimore
    jesus has persisted despite the vitamin pills
people take to make him go away
    he hides in the attic despite
the songs people sing to make him come down
    he is so tiny, he can barely be seen

in a dream, jesus drives
    a stolen jeep over the bumpy streets
of half jerusalem, half seattle
    children pelting him with hard candy
and when soldiers try to get him into selfies
    cellphones explode in their hands

when I see jesus, he's so tiny he's not even there
    he's a glimmer on the surface of a lake
the reflection of a dragonfly, or a
    ripple where a water strider
used to be, and maybe it's a sin
    but I don't really need jesus
to be or do
    anything more than this
to which jesus says
    cool

# God #7: The Last Communion

god is brutal
   like the sun, complex
      like a pomegranate, loopy
like an electron

like my
   chihuahua-abusing
      refrigerator-shaped ex–
new york city
   cop next-door neighbor, god
      is large, contains
multitudes
   like

an elephant, god
   is community-minded
      god sprawls
like ivy, intractable
   and intense, a threat
   to the stability

of architecture, like
   the mango-thieving monkeys of mumbai
      or the raccoon
who dismembers a crayfish in a
   streambed, god
      is almost human

like a squirrel, god
   exudes tragic charisma
      god is serene

like a wheel of cheese
 diabolical like a fork
like tang, the
 orange-flavored
  instant beverage
made famous
 by astronauts, god
  can be reconstituted
with water—
 just one molecule
  does the trick

# The Man Who Fell in Love with a Tree

*Unworldly love*
*that has no hope*
        *of the world*

        *and that*
*cannot change the world*
*to its delight—*
*~William Carlos Williams*

A man falls in love with a tree, a crabapple tree in his backyard, and can think of no other. Enthralled by its unique tangle of twig and branch, elated by its leafy murmuration, he tells the tree of his feelings. The crabapple tree is flattered but noncommittal. The man is not discouraged.

The man who falls in love with a tree is no fool. He knows issues will come up. Age issues: The tree is twice as old as he is. Height issues: The tree has a good twenty feet on him. To say nothing of religion or family reaction.

The man wants to run away with the tree, but the tree remains firmly rooted. The tree says that for the man's idea to progress, he would have to become a tree. The man is open to this.

A man vows to become a tree. If not in this lifetime, then in the next. He reads up on photosynthesis, osmosis, mythology. He watches instructional videos, prepares the necessary paperwork. Other trees say, you're overthinking this, it all comes down to practice. The man practices. He digs his toes into the dirt, strikes a treelike pose. A sparrow lands on his wrist.

His friends don't get what he sees in the tree. It's just a scraggly old backyard crabapple, its fruit not forbidden so much as inedible.

The tree *is* an ordinary tree, yes, but in it the man sees other trees. When he tells the tree, you are every tree in the world to me it's true—mesmerized by the crabapple's form he sees beyond it.

He sees a madrona twisting on a cliff above the sea. A sequoia scraping the clouds. A banyan tree festooned with ribbons encircled by dancing villagers. He sees trees of Africa and Alaska, trees full of marmosets and mangos and macaws.

The man stands next to the tree and gets gnarly, feels tiny buds pushing through his fingertips. The tree says, you're standing too close.

Once there was a man who fell in love with a tree, a man who decided that he did not need his human life, but would rather be a tree. He tilts toward the rising sun, inhales the light, and is satisfied. On his shaded side, a pale moss is sprouting. He knows it is difficult, this love, but he believes they can make it work.

The tree is flattered but noncommittal.

# Country Without Dance

*After Lorca's "City Without Sleep"*

Election Night, 2016, and no one is dancing in America
Nobody is dancing, not one person
Nobody slips under the spell of a rock-steady groove
No one sways like a solitary reed in a lagoon
No one stumbles upon ecstasy mid-dosido
Or slow dances to the static of the broken radio
No cheeky threesome glides across the gymnasium floor besieged
   by giggles
No one wiggles a big toe expressively or gesticulates with mysteri-
   ous pizzazz
Nobody tangos with a parallel self in tragic intimacy
No one is dancing, no one!
No one dances in America tonight

In the streets, there is no dancing
No one is dancing in Chicago or down in New Orleans
No one is dancing in Philadelphia, PA, or DC
No one is dancing in the Motor City

The musicians hit the right notes but the notes do not respond
The red shoes are lined up at the door but go no farther
Snowflakes fall, but in a graceless plummet, devoid of flutter or
   whirl

Even the victors, the ones who would be dancing
Feel bereft, empty, inert, and they do not dance
They are no closer to dance
Than a rotting flounder in a fishmonger's trash

Nobody is doing the boogaloo, nobody is twisting the night away
Nobody is making it by shaking it
No one struts like an astronaut in reverse
No one flows like the river inside the river
Nobody makes like a snake or a monkey, a mighty oak or a cloud
    of smoke
No one is getting down—they are already down, too low to go
    lower
No one is dancing, no one

Out in the graveyard, the corpses hear a rumor
That there's a band coming to play just for them
No one loves to dance more than the dead
But tonight they just aren't feeling it
Tonight even the dead
Feel the life's been sucked out of them
Sucked out of the marrow of their bones

America will dance again soon
With fury and with fight
But not tonight
Not one person—no one—
Is dancing in America tonight

# Heart of a Poet

The heart of a poet is smaller than the liver of an architect, but
     thirteen times the size of a policeman's badge.
It weighs the same as a wolverine's brain or the thumb of a giant
     or a medium coke.
Although sometimes hobbled by melancholy, the heart of even an
     average poet generates enough electricity to power a city the
     size of Troy, New York, or Coeur d'Alene, Idaho.

While the poet's heart is oblivious to the passing of centuries and
     eons,
The change of seasons is another matter, often inspiring a grief that
     approaches ecstasy, and an obsession with the smell of dirt.
Most poets are of the animal kingdom, but the heart of a poet is
     closely related to certain carnivorous flowers,
Covered with sticky nodules and translucent filaments, it emits ul-
     trasonic syllables of primeval fragrance.
It's an eye, a nerve, a flame.
It's a muscle and a metronome.
The heart of a poet is a meandering river, and is also a raft that
     floats on the river. The heart of a poet
Is older than Egypt, permeable and amorphous,
     it's a luminous being of the swamp, including its tentacles, and
     root hairs, it's the same size as Brazil.

If it grows too large, the heart of a poet may need to be trans-
     planted,
A delicate operation best performed in the earliest days of spring
     when the heart still brims with the darkness of winter,
But has not yet been crushed by the cruelties of April.

# The Poem Not There

I am pulling pages, ripping pages, flinging pages, out of folders,
    out of notebooks, I am stumbling, I am staggering, after crum-
    pled wads of paper as they tumble across the high windy desert
I am diving headfirst into, I am disappearing into, the glove com-
    partment of the runaway blue sedan as it careens from
    nowhere to nowhere
I am jogging with frantic facial expression across a leafy college
    campus whose sole purpose is to not contain what I am looking
    for
I am looking for the poem that is not there

I am rummaging through the recycling bins of funeral homes, I
    am shaking out boots and boxes and bottles
I am memorizing dictionaries of animal language, eavesdropping
    on conversations in bumblebee, moth, and raccoon
I am transcribing the murmurings of dust bunnies and discredited
    saints
I am evacuating the contents of my mind to discern more clearly
    its innate contours
But the poem I am looking for is nowhere to be found

I *do* have the poem of thirty silver coins echoing cacophonously in
    the clothes dryer
I have the ballad of the eloquent earthworm and the lament of the
    alcoholic priest
And *this* poem, the one that expounds upon the silence of an ob-
    solete map
And *this* poem, the one that was chiseled on each of nine identical
    tombstones for nine dead babies
And I have this, the poem of the open birdcage door
I have all these poems and more

While the poem in question trembles behind some unseen other
   door. So . . . last night I had a dream that I was with Bob
   Dylan and we were standing on a bridge in Mississippi and we
   were throwing something off it—I believe it was a box of har-
   monicas—and I wrote a poem about it
But that poem is not the poem I need right now

I have *this* poem, a woman with a pink Mohawk sitting in a shaft
   of moonlight as it filters through a stained-glass window in a
   mosque in Istanbul
But this is not the poem I'm after

I am rooting through envelopes and computer files, taking photo-
   graphs of chicken bones and wolverine scat, I am opening up
   the stomachs of alligators and sharks, I am decoding vapor
   trails in the Arctic sky
In the basement of a church I used to attend, I find a locked trunk,
   and fortunately I have a stick of dynamite to blast it open
And inside the trunk is a single gold tooth and I can see that
   something is etched in tiny letters
A poem of some sort, yes . . . but no

One poem waddles across the freeway, barely escaping death
One poem hovers above an exotic junkyard where battered meta-
   phors mutate in a toxic stew
I have the poem in which time speeds up, life goes by, you fall
   down a laundry chute and bam, that's the end of it
I have poems of blurry pronouns with bloodshot eyes who prowl
   the lonely salt flats of the moon and yodel

This poem I knew was terrible as soon as I wrote it and upon
   reading it later, realized was much worse
This one is a good poem, a clever poem, a poem that does what I
   tell it to
But not one of these is the poem I'm after

Just outside my room, there's a crowd forming, you could even
    call it an angry mob, and I know what they want, I'd love to
    give it to them, but I just can't put my hands on it

I can see poems with decaying teeth weeping in kitchens
I have poems that google themselves to see if they've already been
    written
I have poems soaking in the kitchen sink, poems hiding like lice in
    the shaggy coat of a dog
Wishy-washy fishy poems swaying listlessly at the bottom of
    muddy rivers
I have crude barbaric failed poems bellowing sarcastic versions of
    themselves as bonfires rage and whiskey is guzzled
I have poems within poems, odes wrapped in sonnets, ensconced
    in haiku
I have seductive, almost soundless, almost invisible grooves
    sprawling on textured paper and ascending into the ether
Where they impersonate but ultimately obscure the object of my
    search
I squint and sniff, I perk my ears, the hairs inside my nose are tin-
    gling, I lick my lips and can almost taste it
But the poem I am looking for, persistently, eternally, necessarily—
That poem is nowhere

# The Last Normal Year

The last normal year was just like the years leading up to it only
  more so.
It was the three hundred and nineteenth year of the eighteenth
  century, the most average and futuristic episode of the medie-
  val era.
Two blue jays yammered from a rooftop, a bomb whistled over a
  playground.
A landmine dozed in a rice paddy and dreamed of the secret war.

It was the eight hundred and fourth anniversary of the great
  breakthrough, the latest installment of the glorious snafu.
Old rock and rollers met at a secret location and plugged into the
  trees.
A human ear skittered across a muddy river, a three-eyed fish re-
  cited a haiku on TV.
They asked if I was a robot. I said I was not.

Old rock and rollers met at a secret location and plugged into the
  trees.
Zinnias, kale, and tarragon whirled out of the earth, a bullet
  whizzed across a playground.
I said I was not a robot. Could I prove it? I wasn't sure.
In my dream, a headless woman juggled lemons on a fire escape.

Soup simmered on the stove, the voice of Lucinda Williams sing-
  ing "Man Without a Soul" wafted through the house.
It was the year technospeak, legalese, and psychobabble finally
  merged into one impenetrable mass of gobbledygook.
A congressman went on TV to denounce rumors that he was a
  cow, not a man, but only the cows were persuaded.
The fine, beautiful people had us surrounded, and they were clos-
  ing in.

The last normal year was the dawn of whatever, the final collapse
of why not.

It was the golden age of kids in cages, the heyday of exploding
heads.

At the arts center down the road, Tibetan monks in animal masks
danced and drummed in honor of the ongoing annihilation/
rejuvenation of the cosmos.

Geneticists transmogrified DNA from a fossilized eyelash into a
living, breathing woolly mammoth.

Would this be the year the meek inherit the earth? Cockroaches
and Norway rats calculated the odds and made their wagers.

Studies showed the not-insane portion of the population was pos-
sibly as high as 63 percent but only the insane believed it.

It was the year the island of floating plastic officially displaced
Asia as the world's largest continent.

And every night, enormous agglomerations of imaginary wealth
migrated from one spectral region to another and somehow
ruled the world.

The fate of the planet was coming down to a wrestling match be-
tween Genghis Khan and Calvin Coolidge.

Cockroaches and Norway rats calculated the odds and made their
wagers.

If your head exploded, no problem, replacement heads were never
more available or affordable.

I'm not a cow, protested the esteemed congressman.

As Genghis Khan and Calvin Coolidge squared off in the ring,
studies showed the not-insane portion of the population was
possibly as high as 49 percent.

In other words, the good old days.

A headless woman juggled lemons on a fire escape, somebody's
ear skittered across a muddy river.

The only thing which kept us going, the one thing we knew for
   sure: It had to stop.

Day by day, my signature ceased resembling itself, the whorls of
   my fingerprints faded.
The last normal year dragged on for eons and when it was over no
   one remembered a thing.
The super-continent of plastic glimmered on every horizon.
Woolly mammoths blocked traffic in Buenos Aires.

At the arts center down the road, Tibetan monks passed out zip-
   lock baggies of colored sand, mementos of a recently
   annihilated cosmos.
Pathogens and ghosts, sequestered for millennia in the Antarctic
   ice, came burbling out of the depths and floated into the sur-
   face world.
The one thing we knew for sure, and on which we could
   agree . . . actually, there was no such thing.
I emptied my baggie of colored sand in the garden and hoped for
   the best.

The last normal year dragged on for eons and when it was over no
   one remembered a thing.
It was the last hurrah of our fabled dominance, the five hundred
   and seventy-seventh anniversary of the great breakthrough.
A landmine dozed in a rice paddy and dreamed of the secret war.
Two blue jays yammered from a rooftop.

# I Pledge Allegiance to the Cloud

I pledge allegiance to the solitary lavender cloud hovering in the
   western sky and to the entire etheric cloud realm for which it
   stands
I pledge allegiance to the Pacific wren, who (no offense) I like
   more than the flag, and whose mad chortling song has no
   bursting bombs. I ask not what the wren can do for me—I
   know it will do nothing. I ask not what I can do for the
   wren—better to just leave it alone
I pledge allegiance to the garden in winter, to soggy cardboard and
   the earthworms writhing beneath it, I pledge allegiance to the
   weeds and to the last few scraggly leaves of chard and kale
   twisting above the dirt
I pledge allegiance to the shattered terra cotta pot, the plastic ID
   tags of last year's starts, and the broken stalks of volunteer sun-
   flowers
And I pledge allegiance to the state of deep trance and wonder-
   ment, and to the myriad manifestations which it engenders,
   one madcap confederation, under the influence, with poetry
   and bedazzlement for all

# Next-Door Neighbor

There he is, the next-door neighbor
Standing in the backyard, just kind of
Staring off, the way he does
Hey how's it going? I shout
Not bad, he shouts back, how's it going with you?

I like the next-door neighbor just fine
But some of the other neighbors have issues with him
Don't trust him
They say he sticks them
In his weird poetry without permission
And that once they are in the poems
They are portrayed in a negative light

I assaulted a marmoset in a sonnet, said one neighbor
I lost a philosophical argument with a cinder block, said another
The man who single-handedly triggered the collapse of civilization
    was clearly based on me, said the guy across the street

I actually think the next-door neighbor
Might be some kind of visionary genius
If he wants me to be in one of his poems
I'd be honored
Besides if he does cast me as
Oh, some kind of
Psychotic dystopian henchman
I'd never know about it
I haven't read a poem in fifty years
Don't expect to read one anytime soon
I avoid poetry like
Well, I don't want to use a cliché, but you get the idea

# Ballad of the Dead Horse

The dead horse gallops on.
Even after, or possibly because of, repeated beatings, the dead
    horse gallops on.
The dead horse has barely eaten for days, its mangy coat is spat-
    tered with mud and blood.
Is the dead horse a political statement? a religious allegory? just a
    matter of semantics?
If the dead horse is supposed to symbolize something other than
    itself, it has no idea what.
The dead horse gallops on.

The dead horse gallops past racetracks and glue factories, over
    mountains and moons.
The dead horse neighs and whinnies and recites its grotesque
    surrealistic poetry at the rodeo open mic.
Give it a rest! cries the crowd, can't somebody put that thing out
    of its misery?
The dead horse has been euthanized so many times it's lost count.
The dead horse gallops on.

The dead horse shows up in the dreams of little girls who want a
    pony but end up settling for a dead horse.
The dead horse holds a séance in the pet cemetery, summons the
    ghosts of cats and dogs
What's it like, asks the dead horse, to rest in peace?
but the cats and dogs never respond.

The dead horse gallops to the Elysian Fields, where it grazes with
    the unicorn.

Though the world sees one as exquisitely beautiful and the other
  as pitiful,
they treat each other as friends and equals, the unicorn even won-
  ders if the dead horse might be interested in starting a family.
The dead horse gallops on.

Even the dead horse's most notable defenders kick it in the ribs
  when no one is watching.
What is their problem? Do they resent the horse for being dead
  and feel it should be more alive?
Or is it that the horse is too alive and should be acting more dead?
Are they jealous that even an exhausted figure of speech is having
  more fun than they are?

Don't ask the dead horse.
The dead horse has zero energy for analyzing the motives of its
  tormentors, or helping its enemies work out their issues.
The dead horse tunes out the noise and gallops on.
The dead horse gallops on.

# Meditation on My Bare Foot

Not a handsome animal like a coyote or wolf
Not an iconic creature like an octopus
Not an animal that thinks for itself like a bus driver or a scuba
    diver
Not, in fact, an organism unto itself, but a component of an
    organism—
Reliable, taken for granted
Asymmetrical, but intentionally so

Is this the same foot that trod unshod, the sandy red footpaths of
    south india while humongous bats clattered chaotically in the
    bamboo?
Yes, this is that foot
Is this the same humble servant that reveled in the texture of the
    golf course green one stoned midnight in approximately 1973?
    The individual cells are different but yes, this is that foot also
And yes, this is the same foot that dove unthinking into the depths
    of a wool sock one Christmas Day
While the belly and the heart cried out for chocolate

My foot is not a stunningly beautiful dahlia, not the only blue-
    speckled fish leaping about in a silvery sea
Nor is it the green flash that sailors describe, and yet
It sings its own folk song in a voice and tempo appropriate to itself

Is it the other foot, upon which the proverbial shoe *is*?
Will it be the wearer of the other shoe, the shoe that soon shall
    drop?
No, it is not the other foot
It is *this* foot—
        the foot which it is

# Form and Emptiness

Yes, I can fill out the required form but before I do, please note:
all required forms are now required to fill out the "required
form form" prior to being filled out.
Please answer all questions.

What is the function of your form? Are you an accident report? A
job application? A health history form? Are you an alien life
form?
Are you now or have you ever been a literary form such as haiku,
Elizabethan sonnet, or graphic novel? Are you a landform such
as butte, mesa, or plateau?
Are you a thinly veiled form of psychological abuse? Have you
ever formed an opinion? Do you know how to form a com-
plete sentence? Have you ever used your fingers to form an
itsy-bitsy spider climbing down the waterspout?
Or did you form a church and a steeple? Did you open the doors?
Did you see all the people? If yes, please list the name of each
person and their relationship to you.

Be sure to fill in all required fields but please note that until fur-
ther notice, all required fields must be filled in with actual dirt
and organic material, and must be used for growing wildflow-
ers and vegetables.
This form will self-destruct in ten seconds.

# Three-Cubic-Yard Dumpster as Nature Poem

I go over to clean up the old house, and the nature poem is there
to greet me.

The nature poem crouches in the driveway on tiny wheels and
maintains an attitude of total receptivity. Made of a green plas-
tic that is lightweight though durable, it measures 80 by 50 by
46 inches.

Like all nature poems, the three-cubic-yard green plastic dumpster
poem depends on precise details. After some deliberation, I
begin the nature poem with a headless styrofoam mannequin.

Line two is a broken badminton racket. Followed by a busted-up
patio umbrella. I give the poem tubes, cables, rusty nails, dog
toys, a defunct vacuum cleaner, soggy sheet rock, and a couple
of old fishing rods.

In the interests of space efficiency, I smash some details with a
sledgehammer.

The nature poem works in free verse, but even freedom has limits.
The nature poem in the form of a three-cubic-yard dumpster
does not accept live ammunition, dead animals, gasoline, anti-
freeze, radioactive debris or space junk—any kind of
hazardous waste needs to be put in a hazardous waste disposal
poem, a separate genre with its own rigid formal requirements.

Though the nature poem tolerates a wide range of approaches, it is
at heart a serious endeavor—to play on or around the nature
poem is to risk serious injury or even death.

As the nature poem fills with obsolescent crap, some might see it
as a critique of Western civilization, or a satire on consump-
tion, but the nature poem that takes the form of a three-cubic-
yard dumpster is non-dualistic, and is not here to judge.

The green plastic dumpster nature poem understands that you might have been expecting or wishing for a poem about a baby owl, or the long-distance conversations between elephants, but this is a poem with a job to do, and it makes no apologies.

# The Big Game

"Are you ready for the big game?" had pretty much replaced
  "Hey, how's it going?"
The big game was all anyone could think or talk about.
All projects were on hold pending the outcome of the big game.
Doctors talked with their patients not about health and sickness
  but the big game.
At the funeral mass, the priest said the deceased loved the game
  more than anything, and people nodded as if that were a good
  thing.
At the bird feeder, blue jays and hummingbirds put aside their dif-
  ferences to discuss which game plan would be most successful.

The head of an owl swiveled in my direction and instead of saying
  hoo, asked if I was ready.
Wind howled through the gutters asking the same question.
On the day of the big game, I saw a parade forming on State
  Street, trumpets and drums and hula-hoops as far as the eye
  could see.
There was a tidal wave of guacamole, a blizzard of statistics, a
  bonfire of dollar bills.
Through it all, I acted as if I had no idea what the fuss was about,
  as if I were an outsider in my own society, an innocent clown,
  a fool, and I wore my ignorance like a badge of honor.
Beneath my charade, however, the fact is, I was ready.
I had never been more ready in my life.
The big game was not a game at all.
I was the only player and the only one who knew the rules.
I kept playing dumb, but that was just part of the game.

# The Legend of J. S. Bach

J. S. Bach took no breaks.
He played too many notes on too many harpsichords.
Assuming he slept two hours a night,
he would have to have been writing music nonstop for 1300 years
just to get the notes on the paper, just to make the marks.
He never thought about what he was doing, never revised,
he never ate or took time off to
down a glass of ale, or play with his kids.
His kids were basically indentured servants,
toiling long hours for nonexistent wages,
frantically transcribing whatever tune he was whistling or hum-
    ming,
and when the kids couldn't keep up, J. S. Bach enlisted trained
    flies with inky feet.

The songs of the wren and the meadowlark
were originally composed by Herr Bach.
J. S. Bach was the inventor of the synthesizer and the drum ma-
    chine, the theremin and the cowbell.
He pioneered the echo chamber and the wah-wah pedal,
discovered the hemidemisemiquaver,
was the father of the powdered wig.
He was on the verge of inventing
the game musical chairs, too,
but that critical element, when the music stops
and everyone scrambles to find a seat,
was forever beyond him.
He was Johann Sebastian Bach,
the music never stopped.

# Requiem for a Yam

Cradled in my hand, it could be a sleeping hamster or gerbil—relaxed, of a satisfying heft, skin responsive to gentle pressure. But what I hold is not a beast, it's a root vegetable, a garnet yam and it's not sleeping, it's dead, dead and rotten, rotten all the way through.

Its skin is intact, but not for long. The first whiskers of blue mold can be seen forming around its wrinkled snout, as an ashen pallor dulls its earthy orange glow.

This is a yam that will never melt butter, never see the inside of an oven.

It will satisfy no human hunger, author no manifesto, adhere to no mission statement, win no market share.

No one will document its life span with time-lapse videography, nor hang its visionary art on the walls of a bistro.

The most this yam can aspire to is that someone will make it a character, maybe even the protagonist, of a small sad poem, an elegy that might be declaimed before a sympathetic congregation.

But no, realistically, there is no way even that could happen.

section three

# To Make a Poem

To make a poem, you begin with a word. Any word will do.

You could choose at random, but why not choose a word you are
attracted to, or a word other words would be attracted to?

Get to know your word. Enjoy the sweetness of it on your lips
and tongue. Pronounce it so slowly there's barely time to say it
once a day.

Go on a trip to someplace you have never been with only your
word for company. To Oklahoma. Or Lithuania.

Observe your word's body language. See the way it responds to
the presence of petroglyphs and parentheses. Notice the way it
flutters when put into italics.

Create a model of the word in other materials, in clay or the music
of a violin.

Substitute your word for every third word in the lyrics of a well-
known song.

Go into the desert with nothing to drink but the water you can
squeeze out of your word.

Chop the word into small cubes, then reassemble. Heat the word.
Or, better yet, let the word heat itself.

Make a meal of your word embellished with only the simplest of
spices.

Starve the word, until it has no choice but to begin gnawing at you.

Deprive the word of sleep until it crawls into your sleep and begins dominating your dreams.

When you and your word reach this point—and it may take years—you should probably find a second word.

Any word will do but be careful.

This is often when the real problems begin.

# The Old Days

in the old days before everything became so complicated, we
   didn't need a different kind of shoe for every occasion, in the
   old days we were just one-celled creatures, didn't wear shoes at
   all, if we had a nucleus, a cell membrane, a few mitochondria,
   we were set, and in the united states of america back then, why,
   there were only two states, alabama and nebraska, and nobody
   lived in either of them, nobody was going on and on about
   how there's not enough hours in the day, there was only one
   hour in the day and that was enough, and everyone's memory
   was perfect because nothing had happened, and it didn't matter
   that there were no stars yet and no moon or sun, there *was* a
   streetlight and you could look up at it and howl all you wanted.

# Clocks

Although I am not mechanically inclined
    I have lately gotten into constructing clocks.
My models are crude but effective.

Instead of cut jewels and gold,
    I use materials like dead maple leaves
and shadows
      and rotting fruit
pond scum and glacial debris.

My alarm clocks have no bells or buzzers, rather,
    they erupt in silence,
and not at a predetermined time,
    but when
        an eruption of silence is necessary.

My clocks lack the sort of precision that has become so
    fashionable
over the last thirteen centuries or so
    but what they lack in precision,
they make up for in,
      well,
I haven't the foggiest . . .
        maybe rustic charm
or affordability.

I like my clocks because
    they leave a lot up to the imagination.
I like to think they combine the best features
    of a Swiss-made watch
      and a mud puddle.
I keep one with me at all times
    because
you just never know.

# My Life as a Fly

I remember my life as a fly
I remember a small shaggy beast with dingy wings and kaleido-
    scope eyes, I was that beast, that beast was I
I remember my life as a fly, a series of lives as various flies, dying
    as one, reborn as another, and another
I remember reading minds, seeing odors and hearing shapes
I remember hatching from a black egg, on a rotten pork chop, I
    was wormlike and pale, it was a sunny day in Chicago
I remember a dumpster in Argentina, a slaughterhouse in Sicily, a
    pigsty in the south of France
I remember dancing on a soup spoon under an orange moon
I remember the glitter of dewdrops on a spiderweb
And when I met my inglorious though inevitable demise . . .

After a short waiting period, I was reborn a fly
I remember crossing into the no-fly zone and my buzz was the
    only sound there was
I was fiercer than a weasel, more lovable than a mosquito, as mys-
    terious as an inkblot
I hovered above the rump of a water buffalo while a harmonium
    droned
I heckled a bullfrog and harassed a horse
I crawled on the arm of Cleopatra, and into her ear
I remember sharing a ham sandwich with an accountant named
    Sam and thinking "not enough mustard"
I flung myself at windows repeatedly, maniacally, ecstatically
I remember an intimate occasion on the carcass of a goat
I remember pestering a Zen master and, pow, he hit me with a
    stick and I didn't know if I was dead or enlightened
I remember getting a summer job in the quality control depart-
    ment of a flyswatter factory, where quality, fortunately, was low

I remember working as a spy for the FBI, I remember being up-
side down on the ceiling of a gangster's kitchen, thinking "I
don't think they see me"
And in my next life . . .

In my next life, I was a fly—in my next life, I was a laboratory test
fly, I remember electrodes and spinning dials
I remember drinking too much coffee, smoking too many ciga-
rettes, engaging in vigorous exercise thirty minutes a day
I remember radiation, intoxication, sensory deprivation, mutation
I remember dreaming I was a mouse
I remember dreaming I was a fly in a science fiction movie, grow-
ing as big as a mouse, a dog, a man, a house, I was super fly
When I awoke I was a fly, a smudge on a mirror, a zero, a dot
I was a smudge, a zero, a dot, but I was proud to be a fly, aviator
extraordinaire, lord of decay, rightful denizen of the blue
planet
I remember my life as a fly, a fly who dreamed of being a man
Or maybe I was a man who dreamed he was a fly

# I Sing the Body Acoustic


I sing the body electric, I sing the body acoustic
I sing of faulty wiring and feedback loops, of the ribcage xylo-
    phone and the tibia flute
I sing of cowbells, doorbells, and church bells that reverberate
    within
I sing of my head, oh, I sing, my poor aching head!
Head which is an orchestra, a cacophony, a warehouse of balloons
Head which is graveyard and pumpkin, parrot and light bulb
I sing of my freckles, silent as a map of the stars
I sing of my heart, which is a drum and a whirlpool and a flamingo
Of my knee, delicate as an antique violin
My cheekbones which harbor the shadow of unknowable ances-
    tors
My hair, which is its own independent mammal
My nostrils, which flare like those of a cow
My eye sockets, which echo bomb craters
My ears, twin trumpets of negative sound
Left hand, whose most epic poem the right hand erases
Right hand, who I constantly confuse with the left
My skin which has me surrounded
I sing of my feet, my hardworking feet, more soulful than my head
    and arguably just as intelligent
My feet, poor aching feet, bossed around and abused by the head
O heart, you who are drum, whirlpool and flamingo, isn't there
    something you can do about my bossy head?
My head, where the property values have been plummeting for
    years
O my head, my aching head, of thee I sing
Of thee I grumble and stammer and shout
While other voices, their source unclear, can be heard rasping
Let us out, let us out!

# Buddha Rat Blues

*With apologies to C. Smart, W. Blake, and D. Thomas*

Let's say there's this rat.

Let's say he's a happy rat, let's say he adds to the sum total of happiness in the world.

Let's say this rat is indispensable to the web of life.

Let's say he is the will of God made flesh, that he is the servant of the living God, duly and daily serving him,

Or, that even if he is not the will of God made flesh, let's say he is shot through with the electricity of earth and wind and outer space.

Let's say he is well-liked by his peers.

Let's say that by his own standards, he is generous, persevering, and highly literate.

Let's say that he is a patron of rat art galleries and plays twelve-bar rat blues on his rat guitar.

Let's say that the same force which drives the rat's red blood drives the green fuse of the flower.

Let's say that the same immortal hand and eye which framed the rat's terrible symmetry hammered your own bones into place.

Let's say the rat performs miracles, that he is a mystic traveler, slipping in and out of invisible dimensions.

Let's say he is a genius in his own way, has a PhD in applied ecology, knows his niche.

Let's say the rat is inflamed with the power and grace of the Holy Spirit.

Or, even if the rat is not inflamed with the power and grace of the Holy Spirit, let's just say that he is a formidable arrangement of molecules.

Let's say the Year of the Rat was an excellent year.

Let's say that you can discern in the rat, a complex melancholy
which mirrors your own.

And let's say he *is* implicated in plagues and disasters—well, I sup-
pose you're not?
But let's just say that for all his fine qualities, the rat is a rat, an ac-
tual live rodent,
And he keeps you awake, he scratches, and nibbles, he defecates,
he gnaws.
Let's say rat begets rat begets rat.
Let's say . . . there's this rat.
Let's say that you have him where you want him, trapped in a
cage.
Let's say that when he grips the bars with nervous dread, he mir-
rors a nervous dread in you,
And as you shove the caged rat into the trunk of your Subaru,
Going, at this ungodly hour, who-knows-where to do who-knows-
what with him,
You can't shake the sense he's trying to tell you something,
That he is a legitimate force of nature,
That honest-to-God, he doesn't know where he ends and you
begin,
That he is a regular little Buddha beast if ever there was one.

# First Guitar

The first guitar was a cardboard shoe box with rubber bands for
strings.
The first guitar was a hollow-bodied universe of stars and silence
and chaos and feathers.
It was the same crude acoustical device used by the cave people to
claw their way out of the Age of Reptiles and into the Age of
Mammals.
Long before humans came on the scene, the first guitar was
plucked by monkeys, turtles, crickets, birds, and, of course, the
tyrannosaurus rex.
The first guitar was carried to Earth by the spiders from Mars.
Guitars in those days were smaller, but denser, and more powerful.
The first guitar resembled a tennis racket but was not a tennis
racket.
The first guitar was atmospheric.
It appeared in the mind of Picasso and was blue.
It appeared in the mind of John Coltrane and was a saxophone.
It appeared in the mind of Thomas Edison and was a transistor
radio.

Once upon a time, the first guitar was the Amazon rainforest,
sheltering butterflies and jaguars.
Guitar! Six strings still ringing like the six days of creation,
Whose first bent notes did twang, even before the Big Bang.
The first guitar was found under a smoldering shrub muttering the
words "baby baby baby."
The first guitar was a fighting instrument of karma.
Its mojo was working.
Its jingle jangle was fully functional.
Its fever was contagious.

Guitar, conjuring invisible cities, ominous voices, dancing trees,
Lorca's guitar, weeping for the smashed goblet of dawn.
Guitar who claimed a thousand times it was going to Kansas City
but never actually went there.
Guitar who said, "ask not what your guitar can do for you, ask
what you can do for your guitar."
Guitar, whose first album was rescued from the trash and sixty-
seven years later emailed to aliens who considered it proof that
intelligent life did exist on planet Earth after all.
The first guitar was thrashed by a crazed gnostic monk at the little-
known border between gospel and punk.
The first guitar was played just like ringing a bell, tuning pegs
carved from the teeth of a gazelle.
Six strings ringing like the six days of creation.
Guitar, most magical of objects, most mournful and true,
Without which my life would be not my life, but some shoddy
imitation.
The first guitar was a hollow-bodied universe, full of fever and
feathers and silence and stars.
The first guitar was just a crude cardboard box, capable of produc-
ing only one note, but that note, my friends,
Was a real humdinger.

# Ballad of the Rock

*After Lorca's "Casida of the Rose"*

The rock was not afraid of the spider.
Nestled in the garden, in the shade of the plum tree,
the rock was not afraid of the spider, or the earthworm, or the
    skeleton of a cat.
The rock was not afraid of being thrown by an idiot or crushed by
    a machine.
Nestled in the garden, in the shade of the plum tree,
        the rock was afraid
        of something else.

The rock was not afraid of paper.
Absorbed in the pulse of its own oddball beat,
the rock was not afraid of paper or scissors or broken glass.
The rock was not afraid of heights or darkness or the number
    thirteen.
Absorbed in the pulse of its own oddball beat,
        the rock was afraid
        of something else.

The rock was not afraid of the rock.
Migrating slowly through the strata of soil,
the rock was not afraid of itself or of other rocks.
The rock was not afraid of the gargoyle or the asteroid or the grain
    of sand.
The rock was not afraid of existence or nonexistence.
The rock was not afraid of the blue screen of death.
Migrating slowly through the strata of soil,
        the rock was afraid
        of something else.

The rock did not appear to be anxious or paranoid or jittery in any way.

The rock was not afraid of fear itself.

The rock was not afraid of complacency or intimacy or surrealistic poetry or international conspiracies.

The rock was not afraid of being misquoted on nationwide TV, or of the contents of canisters corroding at the bottom of the sea.

The rock was not afraid of erosion or extinction or shovels or guns.

Nestled in the garden, in the shade of the plum tree,
    absorbed in the pulse of its own oddball beat,
    migrating slowly through the strata of soil,
        the rock was afraid
of something else.

# Auto Bio

The battery died but we drove anyway,
Sleeping with eyes open, dreaming while driving, we drove
Deep into the night, deep into the wind,
And when the sun came up, and we were as usual hopelessly lost,
    what could we do but drive on?
One by one, wheels fell off the car.
Dials on the instrument panel spun wildly and we drove
To music, rapid dense music with bass lines appropriate to the
    highway
And then, to the perfect silence of an engine gone dead,
We drove.

We drove from LA to Huehuetenango, from the moon's dark side
    to the burbs of Chicago,
Failed the driving test fourteen times and just kept driving.
We drove with fervor and grace,
Past cornfields, and camels, and alien apartment complexes,
Past skyscrapers and caterpillars and armadillos.
We spent our last eighty-five cents on a styrofoam cup of coffee
    and we drove flat broke—
We were free, like the birds of the heavens, like the lilies of the
    field, like the dangerous whirling stars of the desert sky.
Everything fell apart in Las Vegas, our mechanic collapsed and
    died under the hood, but (!) the car itself was miraculously res-
    urrected, so we drove on.
We drove to Bakersfield, and when Bakersfield was attained, it
    vanished, and we drove to Fresno.
Then a landslide blocked the road, so we huddled behind a bill-
    board and waited for the dynamite to arrive—
We drove!

Grandma stood in the driveway waving "bye-bye."
We drove to the swamp to kidnap turtles and returned with both
    turtles and salamanders.
We drove
Through nowheres crowded with nobodies while clocks struck
    zero,
Ran out of gas, ran out of coffee, drove.
We could have been anybody going anywhere.
We were anybody, and we drove to get
Loaves of bread, computers, flyswatters, cough syrup, to get and
    to have and to be everywhere at once as much as possible.
Wheels fell off the car, brakes failed, there was no gas, nowhere
    left to go, we were being pursued,
Pursued by Communist spies and Apaches and pterodactyls,
Pursued by state troopers, Jack Kerouac, Fred Flintstone, and all
    the ancient hipster superheroes.
Mosquitoes and ants panicked as we approached, many bugs died,
    many, many bugs and we drove.

We drove out onto the frozen lake, cut holes in the ice and took
    photographs of the ghosts trapped in water.
We drove over snowdrifts to the land of abominable snow people,
    and we taught them how to parallel park.
We drove to the edge of a cliff above the ocean and then we drove
    over the cliff, and as we dove through the air and into the wa-
    ter, we kept driving.
We drove to a famous underwater city whose name I forget,
Where octopi entwined our old green Buick and elegant mermaids
    taunted us with cryptic innuendo,
Where gigantic swimming eyeballs paralyzed us with their uncanny
    insight,
We just kept driving.

We drove past nomadic tribes in excellent embroidered clothes
    who stood by the side of the road waving "bye-bye."

We drove from downtown Poughkeepsie to Quintana Roo, from
    Tucson to Tucumcari and on to Kathmandu,
And when neighborhood punks stole the alternator and put Kool-
    Aid in the gas tank and swiped our CDs, we just kept driving.

We drove to the farthest edge of the farthest desert,
Where restless stars whirled dangerously in the sky, and we drove.
We drove as a row of oil wells rose before us and burst into
    flames.
We drove deep into the night, deep into the wind.
We could have been anybody going anywhere.
We could have been anywhere, and we were anywhere,
And we drove to get there,
And we drove to leave.

# Pentatonic Baby

a baby can develop ears
and blood cells, digestive enzymes
and brain cells, dreaming effortlessly
a baby's cranium develops energy
a baby can do everything!

a barbaric crowd demands elvis
a baby can do elvis
a belligerent commentator demands edgy
a baby can do edgy
a baby can do einstein

a baby can
alphabetize, baptize, cannibalize, demonize, energize
accentuate, berate, castigate, defecate, extrapolate
advocate bizarre contradictions, deconstruct existentialism
a baby contains dark epiphanies
a baby contains dragonflies, eagles
anacondas, baboons, chameleons, daffodils, egrets
anteaters, beetles, cavemen, dodoes, elephants
a baby can dig, excavating
archaeological bonanzas, cities dripping emeralds
archways billowing crazily, diamond-encrusted
altars beaming coded diagrams, etc.

and babies can devolve, evolve
appearing bureaucratic, composed, dignified, even
avuncular, babies can deliberate endlessly
a baby can dynamite elephants

asphyxiate barbarians, conquer detroit, even
america, babies can detain enemy
agents by concocting dna evidence
    and be careful, dear elders
a baby can detect excrement

section four

# To Sleep

Friends, as happy as I am to be here with you, the fact is
I'd rather be asleep—and I don't mean just a nap.

I want to sleep like a baby, like a man possessed
To snooze, to slumber, to snore like thunder
To sleep deep, but also far and wide
To sleep in every possible situation, sleep on every mattress, on
  every pillow, in every bedroom in every town
To sleep with friends and lovers and total strangers, but also alone,
  and outside of rooms and situations and mattresses
To sleepwalk through the motions of waking life, to doze on the
  job undetected
To sleep a subversive boundary-blurring sleep, I want to
  sleep . . . dangerously
To sleep at superhuman speeds, on jet planes and on rattletrap
  buses, careening across landscapes which are themselves
  asleep, to sleep among squabbling chickens and sirens and the
  clanging of bells
Through festivals, fireworks, and drum solos
To leave one body and to enter another, to fall asleep as a man, to
  awaken as a woman, to fall asleep as a stone and to wake up as
  a flower
To sleep inhumanly, as a cat or a monkey sleeps, to sleep the sleep
  of mushrooms and tangerines, of parrots and bottle caps and
  bones, to turn up as a character in the dreams of the dead
To sleep a sleep too large to be contained by just one body, to
  sleep in ten, a hundred, a thousand bodies at once
Sleep that overflows cathedrals and canyons, to drift off like an
  iceberg or a tectonic plate, serene and vast

To sleep because last night
I did not sleep a wink
Too exhausted to sleep, I stayed up all night, listening to the racket
　　of shadows stumbling through the house, and the idle chitchat
　　of the clothes in my closet
Five miles away, I could hear
A faucet was dripping, a mirror was weeping

Let me hibernate for a century or two or three
Somewhere beyond the clatter and groan of history
Snuggled into the hollow of a mythic oak
A beast in the throes of a feral tranquility

Look, friends, I know
There are miles to go and promises to keep
But right now
I just want to sleep

# New Delhi Haiku Blues

Haiku accost me at every corner. Ominous haiku, aggressively congenial haiku, so many splatters on the wall, so much watery commercial action at the edge of a leaf.

Seventeen con artists all lined up in a row. Seventeen propositions incapable of being refused. Seventeen tourists in seventeen minivans.

Eight million sleeping people in this city. Sixteen million nostrils flaring with breath. Fifty-two thousand four hundred and seven black dogs howling at shapes. Monkeys of precisely seventeen syllables.

A bowl of noodles, a lizard on a wall, the undulation of a mosquito net. On the other side of the mosquito net, the hiccups of the beloved. One detail askew and it all

falls apart.

# Books on Trees

Never believe what a book says
about a tree
because books are made
of dead trees and the dead
are jealous of the living
and do not describe them
objectively.

Books on geology
are more reliable
although the origins of the ink
create cause for concern.

# Newspaper Dreams

*Collage of newspaper article fragments, circa 2003*

Due to a seriously overstocked occupation zone,
we have been ordered to eliminate several skinny languages.
But if we grow, and open fire,
we will be welcomed, whether paid for or not.

We will be welcomed
in the brown fat of animals, and in choppy waters,
welcomed in every known DNA sequence,
welcomed with pressure and density, inside the love we know and
    explode so well,
in cactus hedges and in the sunflower
database, we will be welcomed,
and in collisions and in the future,
we will be welcomed.

And we will be welcomed in olive and maroon
welcomed with riot control canisters, welcomed with
mice and burning tires.

The mummified heart
    will admit a longing for movies and cosmetic surgery.
The boundaries between police and criminals
    will create excellent
        cups of coffee at the bottom of a mine shaft,
but if we frazzle, and shake and open fire,
    we will be welcomed,
        whether paid for or not.

# Try God

Try God was this
old Ukrainian woman
who'd show up every other day or so
to buy onions, carrots, and parsnips,
and to rail against
the great homosexual conspiracy
to the mostly queer produce clerks who
would nod gravely and
assure her that yes, they
too were very concerned.
Everyone called her Try God because
pinned to her sweater was a button
with that slogan.
"I'm all for trying God," I said,
"but what happens if God is found guilty?
Or maybe the button is
missing punctuation
as in 'I get that advancing cosmic justice
isn't easy, but couldn't you at least
give it a try, God?'"
She didn't hear me, of course,
because I'd never
say those things if she were in earshot,
but what she could hear was
the music pouring out of the speakers
above the vegetable case,
a jangly rowdy folk tune from India.
"That noise," she said,
wagging her index finger at the speaker, "is not music,
that noise is the reason
there's so much insanity in the world."

This was twenty-five years ago.
I think she was at least ninety years old at the time.
I heard a rumor she died and was
reborn in her native city of Kyiv,
where she now lives as
a transgender multimedia
performance artist, whose
big dream is
to someday make it
to Burning Man.
If this is true, thank
you, that is what I mean
by giving it a
try, God.

# Monkeys

The government now concludes
We were wrong about the monkeys
We were wrong about the intentions
Of the langur and the rhesus and the howler
We were wrong about the prehensile tail and the opposable thumb
    and the lobes of the brain
To the surviving monkeys, we have apologized
We have released from prison their minor poets
Regarding the major poets, we have issued additional apologies
The new directive is to let the monkeys be monkeys
Accept the monkeys for what they are, not where they fit in the
    scheme of things
Do not intellectualize or romanticize the monkeys
Do not confuse the monkeys with weasels or flying squirrels or le-
    murs or birds
And if it turns out the monkeys are not only our senile ancestors
    but our barbaric children
We'll burn that bridge when we get to it
In the meantime, we appear to be surrounded
That is all
That is all, o splendiferous monkeys of the abandoned city full of
    dead roses in the hyperreal lighting of the crimson daydream
That is all

# The Naked Economy

Once I saw the economy naked and once I saw it invisible. Once I saw a wart-covered snaggletooth beast shivering in a muddy hole, and once I sneaked up on the beast and I bit into its neck, and the beast screamed out and tasted like a fish, a very old fish, a prehistoric fish, a fish that had been rotting since the dawn of time. Once I accidentally became blood brothers with a very old fishlike beast and I took the rage and moodiness of that beast onto myself. And then, one day I learned that the beast was . . . the global economy. Once I had a thought, a deep thought, a wide and far thought, you could even call it an idea. And then it was gone, leaving behind only an outline in the dirt. Once, the economy asked me for a dollar to buy a beer, and I asked the economy for a dollar to buy a piece of pizza and we ate and drank until sunrise, and we fell into a muddy hole. What happened next remains our little secret.

# O Who Did You Meet, My Blue-Eyed Son?

I met this kid who said he'd be my friend for life if I gave him a
   nickel but after a day he refunded me four cents which I agreed
   was fair
Met a kid who was weirdly obsessed with Switzerland, had a cat
   named Zurich and a dog named Matterhorn
Met a kid known as Deadeye who picked off grackles with an air
   gun
Met one kid's mom who gave me a cupcake
Met another kid's mom who roared out a warning
Met a mad child who dozed among the weedy flowers near the
   homeless encampment while paisley tattoos formed on his
   arms and face
Met a glassy-eyed longhair who groped me in a crowd
I met an uncle who showed up one Halloween wearing a rubber
   skull mask and red long underwear, and terrorized my siblings
   and me by shrieking and cackling and jumping on the furni-
   ture, but who otherwise was a very businesslike uncle
Met a Swedish Rastafarian who gave me an apple
I met an antique doll hanging by her hair from a magnolia tree
Met a clown flying over a village in a painting
Met a frog who burned down a city in a folk song
I stumbled upon a nun weeping in a closet
I met an eight-legged horse galloping beside a dark blue sedan
I met a pediatrician who hit me with a hammer before stealing my
   nose
I met an old lady, the grandmother of my grandmother's grand-
   mother, who lived in an attic where she collected dust from all
   over the world and then she swallowed a fly and she died

I met a two-thousand-year-old man dilapidating in a crosswalk
near the penny candy store as the light turned from green to
red

I met an old woman who swallowed a fly and she did not die and
neither did the fly, a woman who went on to swallow a spider,
a cat, a horse, an antelope, all of whom survived, and then a
raccoon and a stone and an octopus, all of whom lived inside
her and she within them, a being of mass and density, permea-
ble and atavistic, of extra bones, multiple stomachs, compound
eyeballs, a woman of seashells and refrigerators, gravel and
flames

I met a maple tree, an antler, a clump of moss . . .

# Neighborhood

My neighborhood where it's five-fifteen in the morning and the
   date is also five-fifteen, and alarm clocks mutter poetry in a mi-
   nor key and everyone is asleep
My neighborhood where dented poems crawl out of silent appli-
   ances looking for caffeine and somebody to talk to while a pale
   glow seeps into the edges of the sky
My neighborhood and its women in plaid bathrobes smoking ciga-
   rettes in doorways and surrounded by light
My neighborhood and its cedar trees, its chickadees, its cacopho-
   nous crows all gabbling in the ancient tongue
My neighborhood and its pirate flags and its prayer flags and its
   pizza menus hanging on doorknobs
My neighborhood and its flags hanging upside down and its earth-
   worms and artifacts
My neighborhood, invisible geography dotted with basilicas and
   pyramids
My neighborhood where cougar, porcupine, and stegosaurus once
   roamed and still might on a very odd night
My neighborhood and its defunct bathtubs full of rocks and dai-
   sies
My neighborhood and its prolonged absence of UFOs—don't
   they know we all love them and want them to come back?
My neighborhood of rampaging deer, cottonwood fluff, curbside
   computers and smashed TVs
Neighborhood glimmering with slug trails and spiderwebs
Neighborhood to which all roads lead, albeit indirectly
My neighborhood, unsung belly button of the universe

93

# The Hole

The why of the hole and the where and the when of the hole were not details I had time for. I knew there was a hole and I knew I was in it. I knew I was the last earthling and I knew they were coming. They'd killed kennedy, and they'd killed oswald, and it wouldn't be long before they'd kill jack ruby. If it did come down to me versus them, I liked my odds. I chiseled my teeth into jagged isosceles triangles and fortified my fingernails with futuristic vitamins and my eyes had fire and lightning zinging out of them. The hole was the negation of dirt, and I was the negation of negation, in other words, double negative, infinite power. I closed my eyes, spun in circles, got dizzy and fell down. The killers were coming and I needed to be ready.

# Abraham Lincoln

A man falls asleep and dreams he is Abraham Lincoln

A man wakes up and he actually *is* Abraham Lincoln

A man sits on the edge of a bed, skinny legs dangling above the floor, bony hands resting on his knees

Lincoln stares off into the dream of Abraham

Where the dreamer raises a dagger above the head of his son, and the angels buzz like mosquitoes in his ears

A man sets the slaves free, still feels depressed

Abraham Lincoln addresses a crowd in which the cadavers outnumber men

A man dreams that his name has been given to a battleship and can no longer be used by him

A man watches as his face becomes the color of money

Silently, the famous beard continues to grow

The long lean fingers of Lincoln curl into the palm of the hand of Abraham

A man dreams he is Abraham Lincoln, then is relieved to discover he is not

Lincoln falls asleep and into the dream of Abraham

A man falls asleep and dreams he is Abraham Lincoln dreaming he is someone else, Abraham Lincoln falls asleep

# The Beans

My wife cooked up a big pot of beans but she didn't like how they
turned out

Don't worry, I said, I think the beans are good and I will eat them
and they will not go to waste

When, she said, when are you going to eat the beans?

I will eat the beans, I said, at every opportunity

I will eat the beans for breakfast with eggs and tortillas

I will eat the beans for lunch accompanied by rice

At dinner, I will eat only beans

I will eat the beans between meals and I will eat the beans for des-
sert

Even if I am running late, I will always make time to eat at least
one bean

I might even add a few new beans so the original beans will last
longer

I will never get tired of the beans, but if I do get tired of them, I
will go to sleep

And I will eat beans in my dreams

Don't worry, I said, I will eat the beans and they will not go to
waste

The beans are good, and I will eat them

# Mammal

Up until now, and even now, I have always considered myself a
mammal

I have always considered myself a member of the mammals, a
large complex mammal of North America, and I have lived
with confidence of my membership

I have always considered myself one of North America's more
complex life forms, and I am musical and mindful of the con-
ventions of grammar and spelling, and I devour elaborate
sandwiches which I myself have designed

And I am loyal to blood type, and to the brotherhood of the
warm-blooded, and I am grateful for the wisdom contained in
antiquated DNA

And I have nothing but respect for the silence of stone hammers,
and I have nothing but respect for the allergies of the dead

And I am a vertebrate, covered with fur, and I bear live young and
drink milk

And I am inclusive, and I endorse the rights of marsupials (though
I consider them somewhat marginal)

And my song has been described as a descending cackle of ten
notes, three or four of which sound like someone knocking on
a distant door

Yes, I have always considered myself a grammatical, musical mammal, and I am emotionally supportive of my fellow mammals, as I know they are supportive of me

And when I fall into trance, it is a mammal trance

And when I break into dance, it is a mammal dance

And I have been spotted hunting rodents by flashlight while vocalizing with urgency and vibrancy

And even though I have from time to time broken bread with the fishes

And the reptiles

And the birds

And the amphibians

And the insects

I have always considered myself a grammatical musical North American sandwich-eating mammal

Larger than a raccoon, but considerably smaller than a full-grown walrus or grizzly bear

# What to Do

In the unlikely event that you find yourself in the path of a charging rhinoceros, go directly to rhino attack dot-com and click seventeen things to do when a rhino attacks. You will not have time for all seventeen, so it is recommended you pick one and go with it. For example, number eleven, immediately remove all red clothing, including underwear and socks.

If an opossum approaches you aggressively and starts biting or clawing you, by all means, fight back—if you pretend to be dead, the possum will think you are making fun of it, which will only make it that much angrier.

A run-in with a hostile armadillo, on the other hand, can usually be defused by appealing to the notorious vanity of the armadillo—compliment the loveliness of its snout or the sweet smell of its breath, and all hostility will vanish.

Beware the Komodo dragon, the world's largest lizard. They grow to a length of ten feet and are totally carnivorous. You can prevent most Komodo dragon attacks before they begin, simply by never setting foot on the island of Komodo.

Some visitors to the Pacific Northwest report encounters with polynomial equations containing three or more variables. If this happens to you, maintain eye contact, talk to the equation in a calm voice, and slowly back away.

Never try to solve for $x$, which leaves you vulnerable to attacks by $y$ and $z$, and under no circumstances should you try to factor the equation on your own.

If you meet a wolf in the forest, try to appear larger than you are by raising your arms above your head, and then leap quickly from side to side so the wolf will think there are two or three of you—or perhaps that you are too crazy to bother with.

If, however, you meet a pack of wolves, say, seven or twenty or thirty wolves, these tactics will be useless. Your best bet is to act small and helpless and hope that the wolves, thinking you are an orphan, will take you in and raise you as one of their own.

If you are cornered by a woodpecker, move your arms and legs vigorously. If you do this, the woodpecker will realize you are not wood and you will be safe.

Unless you happen to come between a mother Gila monster and her baby monsters.

In that case, I am sorry to say, there's nothing you can do, and you are doomed.

section
five

# O God

o groove o oscillation o delirium
o grab-bag of destinies
o goo of distinction
o genial oddball dictator

from the grunt of desire
to the garden of delight
from the garden of delight
to the grail of debauchery
from the grail of debauchery
to the grimace of death
from the grimace of death
to the grime of decay

give us, o grandiloquent one
our gob of divinity our gilded directive
give us our dose, our daily due
give us
	garlic orchids dandelions
	gerbils osprey diplodocus
	guitars obelisks democracies
	glyptodonts octopi doorbells
	glue-sticks orangutans dirigibles
	galaxies operas defibrillators
	grant us our gloriously opalescent dreamscape
	our great operatic dazzle

o gruff and obtuse drone
o generosity o delight

# Let There Be Light

*"God said, 'Let there be light,' and there was light and God saw that the light was good, and he separated light from darkness."*
*(Genesis 1:3-4,The New English Bible, Oxford Study Edition)*

God said: let there be luminous energy
    and there was luminous energy
God said: let there be a lack of proper seriousness
    and there was a lack of proper seriousness
God said: let there be a device for igniting a cigarette
    and there was a device for igniting a cigarette

God said:
    let there be waves and particles and coffee with cream
    let there be low-calorie delirium
    let it be easy to endure and digest and low in substance
And all this came to pass

And God saw that it was morally excellent and conforming to the
    rules of grammar
And he separated the blond from the brunette
And he separated the illuminated traffic signal
    from the absence of such a signal
And he separated the nimble and the fair
    from the impure and the shady
    from the sullen and the obscure

# Hotel California

early days of the eternal present
a cold wind rips through the kitchen
aluminum cookware clatters, microbes shiver
consciousness thickens into substance, becomes frothy, viscous,
    gummy, pliable
unrefrigerated tortillas engender streaks of blue and red mold
which flower into distant galaxies
wild tomatoes multiply and mutate, accruing sweetness, size, com-
    mercial viability
the proto-surrealists enter radioland, seize control
of spain, mexico, paris, peru
blue devils roost in the monkey puzzle tree emanating cool
harmonicas and saxophones generate spontaneously
archangels howl in the key of G
consciousness jells and coagulates, opinions proliferate
the cranium expands, the first wolves and coyotes arrive in north
    america
uranium dust covers the hands of the great clock
the jaw of a fish elongates, a monkey's nose hooks upward
a silk scarf dangles from the beak of a parrot
grazes a granite pyramid, dislodges one atom
an aquatic worm thrashes on live video
the yogi's third eye opens like an astonished rose
hospital beds evolve wings and wheels
we snap our eyeballs into place and hit the job market
the zero is discovered, then zombies and zebras
jesus is born with a ten-thousand-word vocabulary
but there's no one he feels like talking to
white noise bifurcates into bubblegum and delta blues
rastafarians confer with cosmonauts over speakerphone
diversified portfolios notwithstanding, we go extinct

many mutations later, we're back
pushing a mop through a grocery store
hotel california blaring on the loudspeakers
it's 1978, it's 10,000 BC, it's any year you can name
it's yet another fleeting nanosecond
in the early days of the eternal present

# Marooned

When I was very young, I was marooned on a desert island, where
    I fell under the spell of a great loneliness
On the entire island, there was only me and this one palm tree
    bent over in the wind
Sadly the waves piled on the shore, and sadly the waves drifted
    away, leaving nothing behind, only me
And I was alone, totally alone, for many years

Every once in a while, a crow circled overhead, and this crow was
    my only companion
Every once in a while, a few school friends *would* drop by
And, of course, my parents and my grandmother and various
    other family members
But everyone who visited soon became afflicted with the same
    great loneliness which afflicted me
And everyone drifted farther and farther out into the open ocean
And I was left with this one bent-over tree
And a crow circling overhead
And distances growing
In every direction

I had absolutely nothing
All I had was a tiny transistor radio
Inside the radio lived a cheering crowd
At the center of the cheering crowd lived the mighty Mickey
    Mantle
And from time to time, the mighty Mantle would paddle out to
    my island
And together we would run in circles in the backyard, swinging
    our clubs and howling like wolves
And though the crowd would cheer wildly

No actual wolves ever howled in response
And this filled me with loneliness
And even the gregarious Mick grew melancholy
And the crowd fell into an awkward silence
And again it was only me
Only me and this bent-over tree

At one point the archbishop came ashore
And offered to me a private airplane if I would perform certain
    acts
Which I chose not to perform
And at one point the circus came to town
Which was not really a town
But just me and a bent-over tree

And at some point, I started sharing the island with an old monk,
    who spent all day chanting om
And I guess there were five or six dancing girls
Not to mention a bounty hunter, who said he was hunting Billy
    the Kid
But other than that, I was alone, completely alone

My isolation persisted until the day the first Chinese arrived.
At first it was just a few, but they kept coming
Slowly I realized the entire Chinese army was invading the island
I had no weapons to fight them, just a few sticks
Just a few small sticks, and a bazooka made from bamboo
And (of course) I did have one medium-sized nuclear device
But I'd sworn I'd never use it.

It was just the Chinese army and me
And this one bent-over tree
And like me, the Chinese were afflicted by a terrible loneliness
At night we sat around a campfire together and wept at the desola-
    tion of it all

There was only me
Only me and the Chinese, and a bent-over tree, and Mickey Man-
    tle, and the crowd, now so conspicuously subdued
We all sat around the fire and wept, listening to the radio
And the harsh voice of a crow circling overhead.

And where our tears fell to the earth and mingled with the dust
There arose a great race of lizards
And they covered the earth with giant footprints
Footprints nobody could ever hope to fill
And they lumbered backward in time and became extinct
Leaving me again completely alone

On the day I defeated the Chinese, I never felt so alone
The crowd stood up and started cheering.
The Chinese bowed down and showered me
With tea and silk and running shoes
And everyone joined in the applause—
My grandmother and Mickey Mantle and the bounty hunter
The archbishop and the dancing girls and the chanting monk
Everyone was cheering, but one by one
They stopped their cheering, and they all began to leave
And the crow stopped circling, and the radio fell silent
And even the bent-over tree tipped all the way over and into the
    sea
Which itself retreated beyond the edge of the horizon
Until there was only me
And I was truly and completely and utterly all alone

And to tell you the truth
It didn't bother me
A bit

# The Four Questions of Marginalia

*Consisting mostly of handwritten notes in the margins of a used copy of* Four
Questions of Melancholia *by Tomaž Šalamun (and ending with a line by
Šalamun)*

to grow into a world
to be forever cruel
to pluck an eye to witness a crucifixion
and then to be crucified oneself
he is secluded, never went deeper
never touched the ground, never found the earth
it's eternal but what does it mean?
he is not really discussing
what he is discussing
he is not discussing an arm
the comedic arm hanging from a shirt, the shirt hanging
from the arm
comedy comedy but then a tribe a religion
comedy of pain the switch from god to people—how obvious!
the inability to hide from god
the number thirty-four is circled
all comedy all commentary breaks off abruptly
yes, nice, yes, conversation, light airy
comical, ha-ha, the beautiful, the obvious
nagging effortless pain
the talk of breathing
and again on page forty-two
listen . . . I am the people's point of view
I am the number forty-two
a cow, the tropical wind . . .

to speak of dead yellow men is perhaps
racist, and with a crooked arrow
there is a cross on page seventy-seven
o ruined monster, you squirm under
the law and the passage of time
frivolity, nature and space, statements and commands
frivolity and pages of nothingness
only the black line under various words
above others
the word rabbit, the snapping of fingers
the bombs are so bright
my tribe has been misconstrued
my final words have stopped speaking to me
and peacefully I kiss the eyes
I kiss the eyes of peace

# The Bird of Pure Midnight

*Featuring images found in issues of* Raw Vision, *a magazine devoted to*
*Outsider Art*

I think it happened back in 1945—that was the year I turned nega-
tive eleven
I was on the road to damascus when I was knocked off my bike,
stricken not with blindness
but with the vision of a weird and beautiful bird

now I have dusted myself off, and the ringing in my ears is gone,
and all I want to do—all I *really* want to do—
is to see this bird again
to summon forth, or, if necessary, reconstruct using the materials
at hand
this one indigo-purple bird
the bird of pure midnight

bird who is both a phantasm and a fossil, both a real bird and the
statue of a bird
memory and premonition intertwined, a bird of ink and shadow,
of daggers and bone
a plywood spaceship with pinwheels affixed, a dinosaur with wings
and microscopic feet
a flying contraption made of thousands of tiny violet flowers, it
will have
a two-hundred-mile wingspan and will include the eyeballs of two
hundred and thirteen different animals
the bird of pure midnight will consist of thick gobs of red and
yellow paint, and I will use a flexible plastic straw to blow the
paint across the sky

where we will live together, my bird and I in a house made entirely
    of buttons

to honor those who have disappeared, each bird will be accompa-
    nied by a ghost, and each ghost
will be accompanied by an additional ghost

they say every good boy deserves favor, but I am not a good boy
up until this point, I *have* been . . . pretty good, but I am no longer
    looking for favor
I want to be the shape who lies peacefully on his back at the bot-
    tom of a riverbed, to those passing by, it will be hard to discern
    if I am alive or dead
I will be looking straight up, watching
for the return of the bird

I will be howling in solidarity with the man who morphs from dog
    to moose to baboon to coyote
I will be squawking as a magpie in the jazz clubs of dreamsville
the bird of pure midnight will incorporate three alphabets, two
    teakettles, and a bassoon
will incorporate four cubic yards of cement, an american flag,
    seven half-smoked cigarettes and one solid gold revolver
elvis and marilyn and the underfed santa clauses of romania will be
    waiting patiently in the wings

they say every good boy deserves fudge—I am not a good boy but
    I wouldn't mind some fudge
do you think I could have just one small bite? and how about a
    bite for my bird, who has been sleeping inside the earth for
    roughly ten thousand years?

they say every good boy deserves feathers—I am not that good a
    boy, but
I *am* wearing my ceremonial plumage
I am getting ready to be the mother
of the bird

# Requiem for a Word

*For Jim Rogers (1957–2012), long-time partner in travel and adventure*

Gone is the word, its imprint obscure, its echoes exhausted
No longer does the moon speak its name, no longer does the sun
recognize its voice, the stars cannot be connected to form it

Gone are its windy vowels, gone its crags of consonants
Gone is the word as pronounced in accents refined and uncouth
Gone is the word when used as a verb or question, as an obscenity
or a term of endearment
Gone are the pronouns that stood in for the word, and the tangle
of adjectives that attached themselves to it, gone

Gone are the legends, gone the glorious lies, gone the madcap
lingo
Gone is the word as pertains to monasteries, doorknobs, and noo-
dle soup
Gone is the word as it relates to avalanches, birds of prey, and ec-
static dance

And all the mouths, the teeth, the tongues, the lips that ever
sounded the word, gone
Gone is the word, dead is the language, extinct are the people who
spoke it
Silent the trumpet, silent the gong, exhausted the echoes
Gone are the tiny bones of ears that vibrated to its music
Gone is the word, gone the going, gone the gone
Beyond all vanishing, beyond all dissolution, gone, gone is the
word
Gone is the word

# Faddlefum Gets the Last Word

*For Kenyth Freeman, aka Joseph P. Faddlefum (1934–2019)*

he says I just realized
I need to go home can you
give me a ride I say
you are home this
is home he says you
don't understand I need
to go home I say
this is your home you
built this house
with your hands he says
I mean home I need
to go home and when I
take a breath
and sigh
and say nothing he
says aha
so you do understand

# Moon of No Moon

*The finger pointing at the moon is not the moon.*
  ~*Zen proverb*

moon of no moon, moon of no man
  moon of no lonesome moon of no blue
moon of no shape no weight no density no spin
  no phase no haze no adjective no eyeball
moon of no peekaboo moon of no haiku
  moon of no screwball no surreal no aloof
moon of no communion moon of no doubloon
  moon of no real moon of no estate
moon of no helium moon of no balloon
  moon of no silvery no light no june
no croon no spoon no cheddar no cheese
  moon of no pizza moon of no pie
moon of no cow no jumped no over
  moon of no pink no floyd no dark no side
no keith no drummer moon of no who
  moon of no crater moon of no dune
moon of no honeymoon of no swoon
  moon of no werewolf moon of no buddha
moon of no vampire moon of no neruda
  moon of no lonesome moon of no blue
moon of no man moon of no moon

# Acknowledgments

Thank you to Lisa Dailey at Sidekick Press for her encouragement, insight, and patience, without which this book would not be. Thank you to Coral Black for the wonderful artwork, and for book and cover design, and to Kaitlin Schmidt for editorial assistance.

My main means of sharing poetry has been live performance, and most of the poems included were first made public in oral form. For providing supportive, inspiring venues, I especially thank Paul Hanson and Kelly Evert of Village Books (and the Chuckanut Radio Hour), Anna and Murphy Evans, and Louis Ledford at Honey Moon Mead & Cider, Luther Allen and Judy Kleinberg for the Speakeasy Poetry Series, and the New Old Time Chautauqua.

I want to extend my gratitude to my friends who have been part of Whatcom County poetry scene and to the entire greater Western Washington poetry community. I don't think there's anywhere with a higher per capita poetry appreciation (and participation) rate. A shout-out, too, to Christine Kendall and the Confluence Poets of the Methow Valley.

Thanks, finally, to my love, Jeannie Gray, now and forever.

Of the poems included here, eleven appeared in the book *A Beautiful Chaos Demands Energy*. Nine of those eleven, and an additional eight were included in audio form on the CD *Bird of Pure Midnight*. "On the Varieties of Religious Experience" was first published by Psaltery & Lyre; "Cezanne's Carrot" was first displayed at the Poetry Booth at Community Food Co-op; "Clocks" first appeared in the anthology *Noisy Waters;* "Books on Trees" and "New Delhi Haiku Blues" were both published through the Sue C. Boynton Poetry Contest.

www.ingramcontent.com/pod-product-compliance
Lightning Source LLC
Chambersburg PA
CBHW071514120626
46550CB00006B/2222